THE RAIL STOP AT WASSAIC

ALSO BY DON BARKIN

The Caretakers (chapbook)
That Dark Lake
The Persistent (chapbook)
Houses

THE RAIL STOP AT WASSAIC

Poems by

Don Barkin

Antrim House
Bloomfield, Connecticut

Library of Congress Control Number: 2020943801

ISBN: 978-1-943826-73-5

First Edition, 2020

Printed & bound by Ingram Spark

Book design by Rennie McQuilkin

Front cover photograph by jimj0will

Author photograph by Eve Barkin

Antrim House
860.217.0023
AntrimHouseBooks@gmail.com
www.AntrimHouseBooks.com
400 Seabury Dr., #5196, Bloomfield, CT 06002

For Alice and Fran

ACKNOWLEDGMENTS

Some of the poems in this volume appeared in *Houses* and *That Dark Lake,* often in earlier versions.

TABLE OF CONTENTS

What you look hard at seems to look hard at you.

– G.M. Hopkins

THE RAIL STOP AT WASSAIC

I. A TENNIS COURT IN WINTER

The Election Explained in Three Found Objects

1. A Rusted Barrel

Their jobs gone south, they hollered and got high
around a rusted barrel from whose junk
an orange flame was lashing at the sky
with the wild punches of a drunk.

In school they'd sung their country as a range
of purple mountains crowned by spacious skies.
Now a fire made their faces strange
with savage paint, while sparks flew up like flies.

2. The Garbage Can

What's uglier
than a brown plastic
trash can
on its back in the road?
But in this republic
we're sworn to stand by
while it rattles and rumbles.

Let it tell the contempt
of the garbage men
at 6 a.m.
Let it tell the glib
mind of plastic
gone everywhere

like coffee in the car.

So we let it lie
in the road all day,
a little in love
with its ugliness,
like a crude remark
that brings us some truth
on its humped back.

3. At a Stop Light

A truck's bumper bore
the dark-skirted profile of
an assault rifle.

More Weight

We shrug at shade like wind or fog, though in autumn
gusts of paper-shuffling in lofty offices
will roil a lawn like God's face on the waters.

True, these don't shake the thrones of thickened things —
a banker's manse sprawled on its throne of lawn,
where heavy elms warn lovers to move on.

They'll fall in time the way all despots fall:
first the midget in his braided tunic,
then his statue toppled with a rope.

And though we'd rather have an apple than
the apple's shadow, it's not wrong to think
how clouds as vast as ranches sadden Kansas.

Elegy in a Puddle

Being gone, he can't see
this inky portrait of a tree,
much less the tree against the sky
which is the limit of the eye,

reminding us that the cost
of Paradise is that it's lost.
While Heaven fitted in a puddle
like a ship is His rebuttal.

A Tennis Court in Winter

The nets are gone – even
the posts that hold them are gone.
Someone is making it plain,
tennis season is done.
The faint lines on the clay
are like ghosts in old plays.
A man with a racquet and balls
would stand like a rusted pump.
while boys breezed in on bikes
making their big figure-eights.
No one need shoo them away.
Only God in his froth
foresaw a topspin lob
in this desert place.
Of course, it was just for fun.
Still it thickened the summer months
with a shuttling of white shorts,
and made the dead air *ponk*.
But the season for tennis is done.

Free Speech

This is the land of bumper stickers —
brazen boasts and sidelong snickers
which gas gives us the guts to flash
as bad boys ring your bell and dash
and poets flaunt their rage in verses
on the bumpers of their hearses.

The Sad Glamor of Traffic

"But where are they going?" he sobbed, although
only in sighs, for the furious glare
of their glassy flanks and fiery glass
rejected all such questioning.
And the other man was just a myth –
as tinsel dangling from a branch
above a savage river seems
a remnant of some misery.

And yet dense traffic, squealing wheels
made him hear his inner self –
a savage god carved out of corn,
who sits in our seat, our deeper seat,
and wills its way into the world.
"Where are they going?" he sobbed, although
he knew that men were primitives
and he was their demon – his one clear flame.

A Wake

I thought a party was unkind,
though no one else seemed to mind

the irony of swilling gin
till late to mourn the state she's in.

Plus, "This was what she would have wanted."
And so we carried on undaunted

until the world began to blur
then vanished, as it had for her.

In the Bowl-a-Drome

If you were Greek, you'd go to a grove,
a sacred grove with statuary
to feel the rumble, the royal anger
of the underworld. And not just the drumming
of an onyx ball on bridal timber,
but the ball coming back, its running up
to stand by your side like a grave valet.

And things at a distance – the clinking of pins
tripped up where they stood and giggling
with sweet surrender. Let it all fall down.
Where most keep score, you do it more
for the love of being shod in motley
rental shoes from the rental counter
like a harlequin. If you wore them abroad

they would make the very heavens giggle,
as in spring the pitta-pat of rain
on your plastic jacket makes you hear
twittering in the tops of trees.
When the rain stops with a thinning out
of what was dense and sensible,
the sky is still a drying sheet.

An Old Brick Shed

But what's inside? A slug of fust,
a wooden crate alight with dust,
a handsaw rotten-toothed with rust,
and an owl-eye of sun gazing
through a pane of cloudy glazing.

A monument to neglect,
its roof is gray and guano-specked,
though with no holes we can detect.
But dust-motes streaming down the sun –
the tears in everything begun.

Kid with a Cigarette

His brimstone wince is telling us
he'll blame us for his silvery corpse.
While an old man with his knitted hands,
in his polished box and boxy suit,
pardons us because he's left
his start so far behind he seems
a battered shoe in highway weeds,
where some young wretch refusing to
arrive in rags gave it a ride.

The Beautiful Promise of Snow

The blessing of the falling snow
was like a ladder let down from Heaven.
We'd hankered for that cloudy castle,
left off of all the modern maps
with Hades and the great whales
to break us of our buccaneering.

Now it falls and falls and falls –
a knitted scrim (but bright, not dim).
While into dusk the blinkered buses
scuffle toward their puddled stalls,
and we pad home in brilliant slippers
to an afternoon before the fire . . .

At dawn it lies like drear decor,
the wreckage of a splendid dream.
Yet for a spell this inclination,
so long suppressed, to lift our eyes,
seemed right as rain, as cows lie down,
and icons roll their eyes toward Heaven.

And This Was My Room

This was my first mitt when I was boy.
I'd pound its pocket hard as a heavyweight.
It wasn't a real glove, more a toy,
but it bore my blows as happiness, not hate.

That snapshot is of Easter. We were four
or five and hunting candy Easter eggs
in our backyard. Look at how we tore
around like roaring bulls on stumpy legs.

I don't know when I got this picture book.
The cover's been torn off, and someone drew
in crayon on the back. I loved to look
at these animals at their lunchtime at the zoo.

But something's missing – someone's used a broom
to sweep away what made this place my room.

Incident in Early Fall

Blondes in heels totter out
on the lawn done up as beams
of afternoon September sun,

while three thin birches at the back
hiss insults with their t'sking leaves
(such flouncy frocks are *wrong* for fall).

Still, leggy beams that cross the lawn
bring tingling beneath the green,
even if their time is short.

Thus a clutch of classy crones
talk trash to no, or weak, effect
on blondes who cross the lawn in fall.

A Deer in the Headlights

When my headlights found the white muff of a deer
lying on her side, I finally got
what Aristotle meant by "pity and fear
at the fall of a greater man," as we were taught,

and had to ask what hope there was for me
when a beast as fleet as snow lay like a log,
whose honest eyes were open wide when she
was walloped by a lady and her dog.

Jogger

His grimace looks as if he'd rather bite
his nose off than grow old. Or call it spite.

II. AN ACROBAT LOOKS BACK

The Death of a Wild Man

He lopes along like one who doesn't know
that where he's bound it's best to get there slow,
always with the air about him though
of heading off somewhere we wouldn't know,
with furrowed forehead, squinting straight ahead
as though he'd had a thought then lost the thread.

In his wake today I loped along
and tried to think the end we dread is wrong,
and Heaven's special ones dwell in a cloud,
which simply thickens and becomes a shroud.
(Though on the day, they'll have him in a suit
so no one can forget he was a brute.)

I wished that once I'd waved or caught his eye,
for him *one day* to recognize me by.

Careless

He could unhappily have sat
in that chic café.
But he stood stiff, so that was that
and she sent him away.

He thought she looked upended when
he swore and stormed away.
But when they sat for food again,
it came from that café.

It wasn't bad, what they had,
and he thought her bold
for giving him what made him mad,
and giving it to him cold.

An Acrobat Looks Back

The mind is the wild rider
on the patient circus pony
which, mindless of the rhinestones,
the pirouettes and stunts,
canters round and round
until it turns to glue,
for ponies come and go.

And the children are no wiser.
But Gramps, who as a boy
cheered the rider standing
triumphant in the saddle
through a sun-shower of applause,
feels that he's begun
to be weary of such fun.

And taking to his bed,
his lumpy clod of bed,
he rides the wild clouds
in his spangled suit of stars
where the Big Top flies apart
like a flapping canvas sail.
For the mind is a wild rider.

Snotty Villanelle

Why should I pick that tissue off the floor
dropped where I would see it by some swine
who knew some things a good man can't ignore.

I do my share, although I could do more.
But strangers' trash is where I draw the line.
Why *should* I pick that tissue off the floor?

I read online about a civil war
where a child was blown up stepping on a mine,
a crime no decent person could ignore.

Then last week browsing in a big-box store,
some mother slapped her child ("I *said* don't *whine!*")
Shuffling past, I focused on the floor.

My parents taught me, "Always hold a door."
Everyone has his virtue, and that's mine.
Such customs it's just vulgar to ignore.

Some days I let the side down, that's for sure.
But mostly not. Which is why it's fine
I left that sticky tissue on the floor.
Plus, there are things a good man *should* ignore.

Retirement Benefits

Having lost my list of things to do
I thought to take my walk, and being shy
when someone passed I'd stoop to tie my shoe –
to flash a sapless smile would be a lie.

Though I don't know what one more lie would hurt.
Life is mainly lying once we're grown . . .
lies on lies, the way a dog kicks dirt
to hide his shiny prize, a hollow bone.

And bones just rust – our end to being sly.
Which must be why the graveyards seem so dead:
our maws are all too jammed with dirt to lie.
And everything we cared to say's been said.

As We Age

She cursed our doorway with her frown.
"We're selling and moving out of town
to Florida to be near our son –
not the doctor, the other one."

Last fall, a chill wind came to tell her,
Leave your storm-door in the cellar,
trade your maple-shaded street
for a beach that burns your feet.

Now like chattel jammed below-decks
who tug at cuffs around their necks,
she grimaces and twists her rings
then sails away to the edge of things.

The Ruins of the First Private Pool in This City

At one end deep as bulkhead steps,
its bottom batched with Roman scraps,
this ruined pool recalls those gods
who fluttered down like furling leaves
when Heaven's winds were shuttered-up.
Here once a wife concealed her curls
beneath a creamy rubber cap
and slipped from shadow into shadow,
elusive as a swift or nymph
where shaggy oaks waved strangers off.

If now a silver chain-link fence
makes the place a horrid hole,
this opulence in cement
which once contained a bright content
still calls suave gods of banking back.
To you, the grimy white walls say,
"Nothing noble ever goes
astray from such a shapen place,
and we only guess how dangerous
the deep end was in vivid air."

The Park Committee's Placards

As for littering, it is not open
to discussion. But consider the snug
nests of empties in their sacks,
the savaged wrappers of cigars,
condoms, and candy cast away
in an impulse of delight.

When the lady passed us on the path,
we greeted her with a bird's song –
with the bright trills of nervous birds
we greeted each other. All day our songs
went 'round in rounds, while men slept in
in rented rooms and woke to thunder.

Antique Colonial w/ New Kitchen

The columns make him feel well-bred,
though *circa* makes him scratch his head.
The widow's walk makes her sigh
when he's away, she can't say why.

Odysseus built his wedding bed
from an olive tree that wasn't dead,
so while he roamed a leaf would stroke
her cheek each dawn when she awoke.

Why Old Men Should Be
Neither Sad nor Happy

Sometimes now I think
of my mother at the sink,
tapping at the pane
if it began to rain,
or sometimes just to wave
as she can't from her grave.

Though nothing is destroyed
to vanish in the void,
soon my crumbs will leach
down runnels beyond reach
where they'll forget their name
and mine were once the same.

Which makes me wish I'd smiled
when I was young and wild
at the love I knew
was a witch's brew
of mother's milk and blame
of men who take your name.

How it Happened

That day we were lounging in beach-chairs out back
with a brew and the mellow autumn weather
smoothing our brows which were wrinkled with
the usual worries. And then it was chilly
and dim as a sullen dusk in December.
A big silver blimp had covered the sun.

For a moment, it seemed like a laughing man –
not laughing exactly but bouncing around
like a Macy's Day clown, his mouth a black maw,
and a loud-hailer braying, *I have arrived!*
The sun made an orange corona around
that extravagant gasbag. Our dim neighbor giggled.

These days we mostly mope in the den
with the lights left on. We wince at the news,
then make jittery jokes, and go back to our bills.
But our hearts go out to the starving ones,
to the permanent poor with their kwashiorkor,
while we have so much. And now we have him.

Two Religious Still-Lives

How light will enter a room
and stretch carelessly across
a table and a wall
carrying the cross
of the window frame
as lightly as a young
nun her glum habit.

Or the crack of wild laughter
down the hall at work
that splits apart the low
gray weather of the week,
the long gray cloud
we carried on our back
to Friday – our glum habit.

Deus Ex Diorama

In the dim museum
a nook holds what you'd see
if you dove beneath the scum
beneath a sunken tree.
Your eyes are quickly filled
with minnows playing dodge
and beavers as they build
a weedy dam or lodge.
Lonelyish and glum,
you haunt the lively scene
until your eyes become
adrift in algae green.

A tiny painted bird
dots the canvas sky,
too distant to be heard
if it were to cry.
The bird will never dive
down where turtles creep.
As long as it's alive
the dot of paint must keep
its path across the sky
and never reach its nest,
the canvas can't say why.
Just, *somebody knows best.*

Another Argument

The sound of my heart breaking
was constant in those days,
like plant life crackling
under someone's brash tread
on the forest trail.
On the other hand,
plants die every day
on dusty windowsills
high up in the heart
of that famous city,
with many-tonned
steel girders swinging
across the spiky skyline,
and it isn't nothing.

Waiting

The stranded mind scans the mastless sea
waiting for the doctor to be free,
and meanwhile wondering what white-coated
sleight-of-hand revives the tired or bloated
beyond that silent door? The more you wait
the more you dream its magic must be great.

And dream where there is magic that can cure,
a silent world lies leagues beneath the roar
of shuttling time where nurse and doctor stride
through oozy woods remote from wind and tide,
and lit like milk – or what is waiting for?
So Newton, picking shells up from the shore
"while seas of truth spread out in front of me,"
yawned and blinked into infinity.

III. THE IGNORNCE OF THE ANCIENTS

What We Look at Hard

At dawn the street looked like a barren shore
the tide had tugged the sea from like a sheet.
I paused before the shut face of a door
that breathed, *There never was a real street.*

I'd heard this whisper since I knew my name,
and wondered whether everybody knew,
and if a child would be held to blame
for blurting out, "The world – it isn't true!"

But now it didn't bother me a bit
a wooden look was all the nod I'd get
(though plenty to upend my native wit).
Plus who was there to tell? And what? And yet.

A Son's Song

Since God had knocked his family flat
he knew that as the youngest son
he was their only hope and that
he'd have to fix what God had done.

He knew no charm to right the wrong
until one day he found his aim
and broke out in the kind of song
that gives a family back its name.

But a family can't change its fate
because a son breaks out in song,
which anyway came far too late
and blessed their hearts for being wrong.

Time Doesn't Run

Huck and Jim drift downstream towards truth
and freedom. A dragonfly weaves north.
In his splintered shanty, Pap wakes up.
Since Huck is drowned, he gets drunk and musing,
loops the loop Herr Einstein will loop sober.
There will be a war. He'll die drunk.
The years don't run, neither south nor north.

Icarus and Daedalus

Daedalus had brought his son
with him to Crete to try
the family business and have fun.
Yet still the boy would sigh,

"Dad, why build a prison for
the king's unhappy son?
If I'd been born a minotaur
is that what you'd have done?"

So when his father warned him, "Boy,
you must not fly too high!"
he thought it was to kill his joy
in conquering the sky.

When Daedalus saw him near
the sun, he howled, "Come back!"
And Icarus blushed to hear
that heart of marble crack.

Five on Poetry

1. A Defense of Poetry

I'm running in the leaves! she screamed
unnecessarily, it seemed.
But song is what the heart believes,
and mine ran laughing through the leaves.

2. Descartes for Poets

Nailing down a flapping rhyme
makes me feel more sure that I'm.

3. A Poet's Nap

I dreamt that beauty flowed directly to me
from common things (like a flower-pot) wordlessly!
So I grabbed a pen, and this is what I wrote,
like a naked man buttoning his coat.

4. Theology for Poets

Like a wall-implying mime,
we hint at Heaven with a rhyme.

5. A Perfect and An Imperfect Rhyme

Sorrow
tomorrow.

Joy
someday.

Cemeteries Are Schools

The stones seem sad, will always seem
as sad as weary pale-faced moons,
where they look out on columned cars
as blind as Breughel's blind buffoons.

Yet time is on their side. Each car
will finally find itself behind
a hearse much like a Mobius strip,
which school kids take to be a kind

of trick, not thirsting for such tropes,
yet count their hours in sighs and moans
in class then on the bus-ride home
parading past those knowing stones.

The Ignorance of the Ancients

The dullest Greek would sometimes spot the god's
silver trident sharpening the scud,
and not the nothing that we know was there.

Or hearing willows stirring in the woods,
hear whispering nymphs. And walking with his wife,
glance up at her face for what she felt.

When the medical student meets his corpse,
the aching odor of formaldehyde
means missing someone he will never meet.

When her phone-call wakes you from your nap,
you stare out at the yard and, listening hard,
find her smile wide among her roses.

And when the small boy eyed you on the bus,
you knew you were the god of something sad.

Schooled

"Well, on that bridge he watched the river run
through stony London sleeping in the sun.
'He glideth at his own sweet will,'
he wrote, as though the Thames had time to kill –
or like a young lad running off to sea,
reminding Wordsworth he was young and free."
"Did you always want to teach?" a tall girl sighs,
and all the wind that filled my sails dies.

"I never did. I don't know why I'm here.
When you start out, you do things on a dare –
to test your strength. And then to pay the rent,
as you kids go to school because you're sent.
Though did you ever wonder how it is
the earth and moon come close yet never kiss,
like ballroom dancers with their distant looks?
That's why we're here . . . Page 18 in your books."

An Unnecessary Grandness

There is no hollow like a lofty foyer,
a glossy hall with nothing afoot
but the far-off hum of the maid and the road.

How much better a hovel. Wouldn't your worry
be less looking out on a dirt yard
with broken toys and a low sky?

You'd prayed to slide down life like a sunbeam.
Better to trudge up creaking stairs
to an attic room that once was the help's,

with a window looking out through lindens
and someone sewing, humming and sewing,
and her husband tinkering with that toy.

Old Age in May

I want to get on with the next thing.
I've had about enough of this one.
Not that I've mastered what we do here.

But it was never going to go so well
for the likes of me, a blunderer
always plunging ahead and complaining.

And please don't blame me for these lines,
originally in Swedish and by somebody else.
Let them go by like a crowded bus.

One last thing. Consider my wish,
but not quite yet. I'll let you know when
with a wild yelp from a pain in my head.

Only not too long. My wife
is a beautiful old woman – a kind of height.
One long look, and we'll make our way down.

Passing Out at the Hospital

It was foolish of me to swoon
outside the room where your wife
was going to die soon
and end your natural life.

But she was like my wife –
big-hearted, a hugger and teaser.
Like me you mined your life
for indignities to please her.

I should have had breakfast before
I came to say my goodbyes,
and like her couldn't stand anymore,
and heard singing and closed my eyes.

Men Spend their Days Indoors like Fish

Depressives love the colors of
the linoleum – bad hamburger,
the blue of a harbor by Monet,
and halvah. Nor do the windows here

admit wind. The building is abuzz,
being regional and data-driven.
The flagpole out front is at half-mast
for the soldiers and such. Its rigging chinks.

It is a building, and it has its reasons.
Though soon swung balls will bring it down.
On a screen somewhere a parking garage
slouches this way. Its flagpole will clang.

The Aftermath

Such noise like lightning
across the years,
and then such silence
on the stairs.

I, partway up,
pricked up my ears.
at her bright sound
across the years –

swept under by silence
which for years
will shape a face
that disappears.

IV. PRAISE FOR THE MAKERS

The Historic House on the Hill

When he looked up from his farmer's field
waving with wheat, the snath of his scythe
slick with sweat, the house on the hill

dazzled his mind like a white flame –
light sent with a will from Heaven
and welcomed with a coat of white paint.

And so, although the joists groaned
and mice ran in the attic and cellar,
when spring arrived he scraped and repainted.

It still winks from its hill wordlessly
through this burnt wilderness of words.
God hurls down His will in waves,

and we gather it on our pale backs
and warmed to order, hack at the scrabble.

Spring

Spring is nothing. It's what we learned to wish for
then came to expect. Best to look away,
to catch it from the corner of the eye
like someone striding briskly from her bath
who glimpses the yellow pitcher in the sink.

But fall wears a flaming pendant at her breast,
which we watch in love with what outlasts a fire –
the dress to drop, the bones come frankly forth,
before the winding sheets of snow. Then spring,
damp from the bath, and rushing off somewhere.

Foolish Song

A man is like a goat hung with a bell.
Or else he's like the ocean in a shell.

A man is like an actor in a play
who never says the things he'd never say.

A man is like the shoes beneath his bed.
Some days he dreams and sends them on ahead.

A man is like a heart stuck on a pole,
a lightning rod for pain its only role.

A man is like a dead man in a box
untroubled by a wrinkle in his socks.

A man is like the village in his dreams.
It's coming dusk. His whitewashed village gleams.

Time the Tyrant

Tomorrow's a tornado, black
with everything today
you didn't love enough to pack
when you went away.

The Show

The curtain rises on a raucous scene
of homecoming, so far as he can glean.
Yet settling in the dark he can't ignore
the feeling he's been in this seat before.

In bed that morning opening his eyes
another kind of curtain seemed to rise
on the scene he liked to call his life –
his house, his work, his children, and his wife,

and everything seemed written like a part
in which you know the things you'll say by heart
with frozen frown or grin, though not quite why.
He let his eyes fall shut and heaved a sigh.

But since this stage is brilliantly lit,
and it's so dark, he lifts his eyes to it.

A Week After the Funeral

The sun is bright and clouds steer clear of it.
Our neighbor's mower makes a steady moan.
I guess it's only right that we should sit
through a Sunday whiter than a bone.

I read a clotted book and make some notes.
The deck is freshly swept, the lawn is mown.
The minutes knock their hulls like anchored boats,
their gunnels rub together with a groan

reminding us that we are rich in time
(hours till lunch and dinner, and then bed),
and that squandering a Sunday is a crime
against the destitution of the dead,

who'd just as soon they hadn't ever died.
Finally the sun drives us inside.

Around the Corner

School-slacked and jacketed
with a toy-like plaid backpack,
the little black boy
waits for the school bus.
His mother (straight-backed,
a bathrobed duchess)
holds hands with her phone.

When a car comes toward him
taking the tight turn slowly
he raises his small face,
and his eyes rise above
the morning pout of his mouth
like a pearly moon
over desolate docklands.

All the stars in the sky
bob in the black wells of those eyes
(his rumpled bed, last Halloween,
and the foggy forms of grownups gossiping
in the fragrant kitchen) as the car corners –
that contains no cousin, is not big
like a bus. Is not even yellow.

Praise for the Makers

On a frozen afternoon
the codger haunts his block,
rolled up like the rug
they propped against a tree
where they bought a brand-new rug.

Thin fingers in a hovel
once wove that threadbare rug.
And who was it wove him?
What fingers in what hovel
gripped a brawny back?

When they roll him like a rug
and lay him in his grave,
his son will lift his eyes
where redbreasts thread their nest
of straw, and twig, and sky.

The Socrates at Breakfast

Their postcard glowed with tulips.
"This time it's Holland?" I asked.
"They went Dutch," she smirked.
"Well, the man lands on his feet."
"You know that he owns nothing."
"And yet he gets to travel."
"Do you want us to travel?"
"No, you know I don't.
Still, nothing sticks to him."
"But what's he amounted to –
at your age, what's he got?"
"Time to pick tulips, at least,
while I'll be at my desk."
"It's a bicycle tour – you'd hate that."
"I would. Still, they're in Holland
and we're still here. You see?"
"I see. So, no to Holland?"
"No time soon," I said.
"Though you know where I'd like to go?
In the fullness of time -- Heaven."
She looked tired down at her coffee.
"Why, I'd even consider Hell,
if that's what I end up deserving."
"No fussing with bags, just your baggage?"
"We burn our hope like jet fuel.
What I'd really like to see
is the life behind the life,
which if not in this kitchen, is nowhere."
"Hell and Heaven are here?"

"Over breakfast, we've been both places,
we've circled the globe of each other
like Puck, or Satan in Milton.
Right now I'm in Heaven – your face
wistful in resignation
is prettier than that postcard.
And now I'm going to work,
but I'll write you if anything's blooming.
There's nobody I'd rather tell."
Two eyebrows floated up
like balloons from an anchored smile.
And glancing my back like a snowball,
"Nothing ever sticks to you, does it?"

Three Straight Days of Rain

I thought, *He's left us all for dead —*
the way He did in Noah's day
when clouds rolled in at dawn to stay,
then rain to make us snug in bed.

Though now the clouds have exited
and left me blameless under blue,
I'd rather know what Noah knew
about our cloudy sense of dread.

As I know clomping gloomily
down the cellar stairs sometimes
in dungeon darkness that my crimes
have finally caught up with me.

As waking up the attic beams
with my heavy gallows tread
on the staircase up to bed,
He's laying for me in my dreams.

Dulled Elegy

Everything survives,
broken toys and lives
in a heap that grows
somewhere above the brim —
those epic boyhood snows.

My brother's gaze was dim
and strangers shrank from him
as if he were a bear.
I loved him like a brother,
and now he isn't here.

Though dumbstruck like the other
mourners (just our mother
and two strange friends of his)
I hear my brother swear,
"It's snowing!" And it is.

I recognize your stare:
the blizzards I hold dear
rage only in this brain —
and the saddest tear
is just as sad as rain.

The Rail-Stop at Wassaic

The last train leaves, and no one comes home to the house,
a darkened farm-house without cars
that sits by itself at the foot of a wooded ridge,
a sofa on the porch, and a clanging flagpole.
Behind it, a ragged lawn wanders up
to a black maw that beckons you into the woods.

Dusk draws on, and the hill grows rich with shadows.
Head up the path, already black at your feet,
and soon you'll be lost, unlooked for and unseen,
and finally you'll have found it, the source of the stream
of loneliness that flows over you at night in bed.
Now, freeze beneath a low bough like a mole.

If you stay there forever you'll never be more alone,
in a place the rain can fall on without thought.

"We Owe a Cock to Aesculapius"

A man should live just long enough
to settle his debts and bring back the books
charged out on his card. No hospital bill,
no burial bill should slip with a shower
of condolence notes on the sunny rug.

And begin again, in light like ice
(with fury in his balled-up fists
at someone's mess), with a plumber's squint
in a jungle of pipes, listen for smiles
in lullabies, to see things through.

After Her Death

Though wooden-hearted, I still have thoughts:
Where she is, she is beyond wisdom –
imagine that! Like the rest of us
she prayed for it. Well, she can let fall
her divining-rod now. Then, on the porch,
I looked up and thought, "Well, she is released
into the blue sky framed
with the blossoms of those tall trees."

Two Incidents

What made that morning different,
we'd made a black guy President.

I passed black people on my street
and didn't look down at my feet.

And once at twenty, drunk on brew,
I asked this wino that I knew,

"What's it like?" And he said he
recalled his dad "dressed to the T

and tipping his hat to ladies *and* gents."
He was drunk, too, so it made sense

that what he had to say to me
was he had come from dignity.

A Day at the Beach

Behind that grassy swell slept the sea.
But first the burning beach. He shucked his shoes
and, sobbing like a raw recruit, shot free
of his parents' power to coddle and confuse.

The sparkling vasty white-peaked sea
vanished at its distant rim like magic.
He squinted at a blur, which could be
the coast of France or fog, which was tragic,

and hurled himself into the surf to drown
but failed and groped his way back toward the sun.
Then mooned that mothering sun and dove back down.
Back on the beach, they'd ask if he'd had fun.

ABOUT THE AUTHOR

Don Barkin has published poems in *Poetry, The Virginia Quarterly Review, Prairie Schooner, Poetry Northwest, the North American Review, Harvard Magazine, The Louisville Review, Commonweal,* and other journals. A full-length collection of his poems, *That Dark Lake,* published by Antrim House in 2009, was a finalist for the Connecticut Center for the Book's Poetry Book of the Year award. *Houses, New and Selected Poems,* was published by Antrim House in 2017. Two chapbooks, *The Caretakers* and *The Persistent,* were published by Finishing Line Press. He has twice been awarded artist grants by the State of Connecticut. He is a former newspaper reporter and was educated at Harvard and Cambridge Universities. He has taught writing at Yale, Wesleyan, and Connecticut College. He lives in New Haven, Connecticut with his wife, Maggie, and his daughter, Eve.

For more concerning the work of Don Barkin, visit
www.antrimhousebooks.com/authors.html.
This book is available at all bookstores
including Amazon.